IT Fundamentals

A Complete Guide to CompTIA A+ and Essential Tech Skills

Rufus J. Andrews

Table of Contents

Introduction _____**5**

Welcome to the World of IT! _____5

Chapter 1 _____**7**

Understanding IT Fundamentals_____7

Chapter 2 _____**11**

Inside the Computer – Components and Functions___11

Chapter 3 _____**17**

Peripheral Devices and Ports – Connecting the Dots__17

Chapter 4 _____**24**

Storage Technologies – Keeping Your Data Safe and Fast
_____24

Chapter 5 _____**31**

Mobile and Laptop Hardware – Compact Power on the
Go _____31

Chapter 6 _____**38**

Operating System Basics – The Software That Runs the
Show _____38

Chapter 7 _____**47**

Command Line and System Utilities – Mastering the
Hidden Power of Your OS _____47

Chapter 8 _____**54**

Virtualization and Cloud Computing – The Future of IT
Infrastructure _____54

Chapter 9 _____**61**

Networking Basics – How Computers Talk to Each Other
_____61

Chapter 10 _____ 68

Network Hardware and Topologies – The Blueprint of
Connectivity _____ 68

Chapter 11 _____ 76

Wireless Technologies and Security – Cutting the Cords,
Keeping It Safe _____ 76

Chapter 12 _____ 85

Cybersecurity Essentials – Defending the Digital Frontier
_____85

Chapter 13 _____ 92

User Access and Authentication – Locking the Digital
Doors _____ 92

Chapter 14 _____ 100

Hardware and Software Troubleshooting – Fixing Tech
like a Pro _____ 100

Chapter 15 _____ 109

Preventive Maintenance and Best Practices – Keeping IT
Running Smoothly_____ 109

Chapter 16 _____ 117

IT Ethics and Customer Service – The Human Side of
Tech _____ 117

Chapter 17 _____ 125

Job Roles, Certifications, and Career Growth – Your Path
in IT _____ 125

Chapter 18_____**134**

Quick Reference Cheat Sheets & Real-World Scenarios
_____134

Introduction

Welcome to the World of IT!

Imagine you're on a spaceship—destination: IT mastery. Whether you're a total newbie gearing up for your first IT job or a seasoned pro looking to refresh your knowledge, this book is your co-pilot. We'll navigate the vast universe of IT fundamentals, covering everything from hardware and software to networking, security, and troubleshooting.

Why IT? Why Now?

Technology is everywhere—your smartphone, your smart fridge, even your car is a mini-computer on wheels. IT professionals are the backbone of this digital world, keeping systems running, networks secure, and users (mostly) happy. With the CompTIA A+ certification, you prove to the world that you know your stuff, making you a valuable asset in today's job market.

What You'll Learn

This book is more than just theory—it's a fun, practical guide designed to help you truly understand IT concepts. Each chapter breaks down complex topics into easy-todigest explanations, real-world examples, and hands-on practice questions. By the time you finish, you'll have:

✓ A solid grasp of hardware, software, networking, and security

✓ The skills to troubleshoot common IT problems like a pro

✓ A roadmap to acing the CompTIA A+ exam and launching your IT career

How to Use This Book

You can read this book cover to cover or jump straight to the topics you need. If you're studying for CompTIA A+, use the practice questions at the end of each chapter to test your knowledge. If you're a working professional, keep this book handy as a quick reference guide.

So, grab your coffee (or energy drink of choice), buckle up, and let's get started on your journey to becoming an IT expert. The future of tech is in your hands—let's make it happen!

Chapter 1

Understanding IT Fundamentals

Take a look around. You're probably reading this on a smartphone, tablet, or laptop—maybe even a dual-monitor setup with RGB lights flashing like a mini Las Vegas. That's the beauty of IT: it's everywhere. From banking apps to gaming consoles, from medical devices to self-driving cars, IT is the invisible force powering our world.

But before we dive into the nuts and bolts of computers, let's get a high-level view of what IT is all about.

What is IT, Really?

IT, or Information Technology, is the use of computers, networks, and software to process, store, and transmit data. But let's keep it real—IT isn't just about plugging in cables and clicking buttons. It's about solving problems and making things work.

IT professionals wear many hats, such as:

- **Hardware Technicians** – The doctors of the IT world, fixing broken computers.

- **Network Administrators** – The architects behind Wi-Fi and data networks.

- **Cybersecurity Experts** – The guardians protecting against hackers and malware.

- **Software Developers** – The masterminds creating apps and programs.

Regardless of your role, every IT pro starts with the fundamentals—which is exactly what we're here to master.

The Importance of IT in Today's World

IT isn't just a career path—it's a superpower. Companies can't function without it. Imagine:

- No IT Support? Offices would be in chaos every Monday morning.

- No Networking? The internet as we know it wouldn't exist.

- No Cybersecurity? Your bank account would be an open playground for hackers.

That's why IT professionals are in high demand across every industry—from healthcare and finance to gaming and entertainment.

The CompTIA A+ Certification: Your Ticket to IT Success

You might be wondering, "Why should I care about the CompTIA A+ certification?" Well, if you're new to IT, A+ is your golden ticket. It's the industry's most recognized entry-level certification, proving that you understand hardware, software, troubleshooting, and security. It's often required for IT support, help desk, and technician roles.

With an A+ certification, you show employers that:

✓ You understand computer hardware and software

✓ You can fix and troubleshoot IT problems

✓ You have the skills to support users and maintain systems

Fun fact: Many top IT professionals—yes, even the ones working at Google and Microsoft—started with a CompTIA A+ certification before climbing the tech ladder.

A Quick Look at What's Coming Next

Now that we've set the stage, it's time to roll up our sleeves and get technical. In the next chapter, we'll open up the computer (figuratively and maybe even literally) to explore its inner workings. You'll learn about motherboards, processors, RAM, storage, and all the essential components that make a system tick.

Quick Check: Test Your Knowledge

Let's see what you've picked up! Try answering these questions:

1. What does IT stand for, and why is it important?

2. Name three career paths in IT and what they do.

3. Why is the CompTIA A+ certification valuable for beginners?

Chapter 2

Inside the Computer – Components and Functions

E ver looked inside a computer and thought, "What the heck is all this stuff?" Don't worry—you're not alone. At first glance, a PC's internals can seem like an electronic jungle of circuit boards, wires, and blinking lights. But once you understand the key components and their roles, it all starts making sense.

Whether you're assembling a custom gaming PC, troubleshooting a malfunctioning laptop, or just trying to impress your friends with your tech knowledge, understanding the hardware inside a computer is fundamental to IT.

Meet the Core Components

Every computer, from a high-end server to your personal laptop, has the same basic parts. Let's break them down one by one.

1. The Motherboard – The Nervous System

Think of the motherboard as the central hub of the computer. It's a printed circuit board (PCB) that connects all the hardware components, allowing them to communicate.

Key features of a motherboard:

✓ CPU socket – Where the processor (brain) sits

✓ RAM slots – Holds your system's short-term memory

✓ Expansion slots – For graphics cards, sound cards, and other upgrades

✓ Power connectors – Distributes power from the power supply

✓ Data connectors – Links storage drives (HDDs, SSDs) and peripherals

Without the motherboard, your computer is just a pile of expensive parts.

2. The CPU – The Brain of the Operation

The Central Processing Unit (CPU) is the brain of the computer, handling instructions, calculations, and decision-making.

Key CPU specs:

- Clock speed (GHz) – Determines how fast it processes tasks

- Cores & Threads – More cores = better multitasking

- Cache Memory – Small but ultra-fast memory for quick data access

Popular CPU brands? Intel and AMD dominate the market. Ever heard of an Intel Core i7 or an AMD Ryzen 9? Those are high-performance CPUs used in gaming, video editing, and more.

3. RAM – The Short-Term Memory

Random Access Memory (RAM) is the temporary workspace of your computer. It's where data is stored while it's actively being used.

RAM's role:

- More RAM = faster multitasking

- Acts as a bridge between the CPU and storage

- Measured in GB (Gigabytes) – 8GB is standard, but 16GB+ is ideal for power users

Think of RAM like a workbench—the more space you have, the more tools you can lay out at once. When you shut down your PC, RAM clears out completely.

4. Storage – The Long-Term Memory

Your storage drive holds all your data—even when the power is off.

Types of Storage:

- HDD (Hard Disk Drive) – Older, mechanical drives with moving parts. Slower but cheaper.

- SSD (Solid State Drive) – Faster, no moving parts, and more reliable.

- NVMe SSD – The fastest of all, using PCIe lanes for blazing speeds.

If your system still runs on an HDD, upgrading to an SSD is like swapping out a bicycle for a sports car.

5. The Power Supply Unit (PSU) – The Heartbeat

Without power, nothing works. The Power Supply Unit (PSU) converts electricity from your wall outlet into a form that your computer can use.

PSU Ratings to Know:

✓ Watts (W) – Higher watts support more powerful components

✓ 80 Plus Certification – Efficiency rating (Bronze, Silver, Gold, Platinum)

Pro tip: Always get a good-quality PSU—cheap ones can fail and damage your entire system.

6. Expansion Cards – Boosting Your PC's Capabilities

While motherboards come with built-in features, sometimes you need extra power.

- Graphics Card (GPU) – For gaming, video editing, and AI computing (NVIDIA & AMD lead the market)

- Sound Card – Enhances audio quality for audiophiles

- Network Card (NIC) – Provides better wired or wireless networking

If you're into gaming, a dedicated GPU (like an RTX 4080) is essential.

Understanding Computer Architecture

Now that you know the parts, let's see how they all work together:

- Power On – PSU delivers power to components
- BIOS/UEFI Loads – The motherboard's firmware checks hardware
- CPU Activates – Fetches data from storage and RAM

- Operating System Loads – Windows, macOS, or Linux boots up
- You Take Over – Open apps, browse the web, or get to work.

Each component plays a role in this startup process, and understanding how they interact will help you troubleshoot when things go wrong.

Quick Check: Test Your Knowledge

Time to see if you got this! Answer the following:

1. What is the primary function of the motherboard?

2. How does RAM differ from storage?

3. Why is an SSD better than an HDD?

4. What does the power supply do?

5. What component is considered the brain of the computer?

Chapter 3

Peripheral Devices and Ports – Connecting the Dots

Imagine having a powerful PC with a high-speed processor, loads of RAM, and a top-tier graphics card—but no keyboard, mouse, or monitor. Pretty useless, right? That's where peripherals and ports come in.

Peripherals are the external devices that connect to your computer to expand its functionality. Whether it's a printer, external hard drive, or gaming headset, each peripheral needs the right port to connect and function properly.

Types of Peripheral Devices

1. Input Devices – The Data Feeders

Input devices allow you to send information to your computer.

Common Input Devices:

- Keyboard – Standard, mechanical, ergonomic, or gaming types

- Mouse – Optical, laser, or trackball (bonus points if yours has RGB lighting)

- Touchscreens – Found in tablets, smartphones, and some laptops

- Scanners – Converts physical documents into digital files

- Microphones – For recording audio or voice commands (Alexa, anyone?)

- Webcams – Essential for video calls and streaming.

Without input devices, you wouldn't be able to interact with your computer.

2. Output Devices – The Data Presenters

Output devices take processed data and present it in a human-readable format.

Common Output Devices:

- Monitors – Display visuals; key specs include resolution (1080p, 4K) and refresh rate (60Hz, 144Hz, 240Hz)

- Printers – Inkjet, laser, and 3D printers for physical documents and objects

- Speakers & Headphones – Output audio, essential for entertainment and communication.

Without output devices, your computer would be a black box of calculations with no way to show results.

3. Storage Devices – The Digital Vaults

While internal storage (HDD, SSD) is built into a computer, external storage devices provide extra space and portability.

Common Storage Peripherals:

- External Hard Drives (HDD/SSD) – Used for backups and extra storage

- USB Flash Drives – Small, portable storage (great for quick file transfers)

- Memory Cards (SD, microSD) – Found in cameras, phones, and game consoles

- Network Attached Storage (NAS) – A storage system connected to a network for multiple users.

Storage peripherals extend the data capacity of a system and allow for easier data transfer.

4. Network Devices – Staying Connected

These devices enable computers to communicate with each other and access the internet.

Key Networking Peripherals:

- Routers – Direct internet traffic, connecting multiple devices

- Modems – Convert internet signals from your ISP

- Wi-Fi Adapters – Add wireless capability to desktops or older laptops

- Ethernet Cables – Provide wired, stable internet connections.

A computer without a network connection is like a phone without a signal—functional, but missing out on the real action.

Understanding Ports and Connectors

1. USB – The Universal Connector

USB (Universal Serial Bus) is the most common connection type for peripherals.

Types of USB Ports:

- USB-A – The standard rectangular USB port (flash drives, keyboards)

- USB-B – Less common; found in printers and some external hard drives

- USB-C – The latest, faster, reversible connector (modern laptops, smartphones)

- USB 3.0 / 3.1 / 3.2 / 4.0 – Newer versions with faster data transfer speeds.

Fun fact: USB-C is slowly replacing USB-A due to its versatility and speed.

2. Display Ports – Connecting Monitors

Your choice of display port affects video quality and refresh rates.

Common Video Ports:

- HDMI (High-Definition Multimedia Interface) – Standard for TVs, monitors, gaming consoles

- DisplayPort (DP) – Preferred for high-resolution and high-refresh-rate monitors

- VGA (Video Graphics Array) – Older analog connection (mostly obsolete)

- DVI (Digital Visual Interface) – A step between VGA and HDMI.

If you're into high-resolution gaming or video editing, DisplayPort and HDMI are your best bets.

3. Audio Ports – For Sound Lovers

Audio ports allow you to connect speakers, microphones, and headsets.

Types of Audio Ports:

- 3.5mm Jack – Standard headphone/microphone connection

- Optical (TOSLINK) – High-quality digital audio (home theaters, soundbars)

- USB Audio – Some headsets use USB for enhanced sound processing

- Bluetooth – Wireless audio connectivity.

Wired or wireless? Audiophiles swear by wired for better sound quality, but Bluetooth offers convenience.

4. Ethernet vs. Wi-Fi – The Internet Connection Debate

Wired or wireless? That's the question.

✓ Ethernet (RJ45) – Stable, high-speed connection for gaming and streaming

✓ Wi-Fi – Convenient, but can suffer from interference and slower speeds.

If you want the fastest, most reliable internet, Ethernet is king. But for convenience, Wi-Fi wins.

Peripheral and Port Troubleshooting

What happens when a device isn't working? Here are quick fixes:

◆ USB device not recognized? Try a different port or update drivers.

◆ Monitor not displaying? Check the cable and switch input sources.

◆ Wi-Fi dropping? Restart your router and update network drivers.

◆ Printer not printing? Check ink levels and reinstall drivers.

Knowing how to troubleshoot peripherals is a crucial IT skill—master it, and you'll be a hero in any office.

Quick Check: Test Your Knowledge

1. What's the difference between input and output devices?

2. Name three common storage peripherals and their uses.

3. What's the advantage of USB-C over USB-A?

4. Why might you choose Ethernet over Wi-Fi?

5. Which display port is best for high refresh rates?

Chapter 4

Storage Technologies – Keeping Your Data Safe and Fast

S torage is where your digital life lives. Your operating system, apps, documents, games, and even that embarrassing old photo collection—all stored on some form of data storage device.

But not all storage is created equal. Some are lightning fast, others are cheap but slow, and some provide extra security to protect against data loss. In this chapter, we'll break down the different types of storage, their advantages and disadvantages, and best practices for keeping your data safe.

Types of Storage Devices

1. Hard Disk Drives (HDDs) – The Old Workhorse

Hard Disk Drives (HDDs) have been around since the 1950s, and they're still kicking. They store data on spinning magnetic platters, read by a tiny mechanical arm.

Pros of HDDs:

✓ Affordable – More storage for less money

✓ High capacity – 2TB, 4TB, or even 10TB drives are common

✓ Good for bulk storage – Great for archives, backups, and media libraries.

Cons of HDDs:

✗ Slow – Mechanical parts mean slower read/write speeds

✗ Fragile – A drop or shake while running can damage the platters

✗ Noisy – Spinning disks and moving arms create noise

Think of HDDs like a filing cabinet—they hold a lot, but accessing files can take time.

2. Solid-State Drives (SSDs) – The Speed Boost

Solid-State Drives (SSDs) have no moving parts. Instead, they use flash memory (like a USB stick) to store data, making them much faster and more reliable than HDDs.

Pros of SSDs:

✓ Blazing fast – Boots Windows in seconds, loads apps instantly

✓ Silent – No moving parts = no noise

✓ More durable – Can survive drops and shocks better than HDDs

Cons of SSDs:

✗ More expensive per GB – SSDs cost more than HDDs

✗ Limited write cycles – Flash memory wears out over time (though modern SSDs last for years).

Think of SSDs like a fast, organized bookshelf—you grab what you need instantly.

3. NVMe SSDs – The Formula 1 of Storage

Non-Volatile Memory Express (NVMe) SSDs take speed to another level. Unlike traditional SSDs, which use the SATA interface, NVMe drives use the PCIe lanes directly on the motherboard for even faster performance.

Pros of NVMe SSDs:

✓ Extremely fast – Read/write speeds up to 7000MB/s (vs. 500MB/s for SATA SSDs)

✓ Best for gaming and video editing – Reduces load times drastically

✓ Small form factor – M.2 drives are compact and fit directly into the motherboard

Cons of NVMe SSDs:

✗ More expensive than SATA SSDs

✗ Not all motherboards support NVMe (older ones use only SATA)

If a SATA SSD is a sports car, an NVMe SSD is a rocket ship.

4. External and Portable Storage

Need to move files between devices? External drives are your best bet.

Common External Storage Options:

- USB Flash Drives – Small, portable, and great for quick transfers

- External HDDs/SSDs – Larger capacity for backups and media storage

- Memory Cards (SD, microSD) – Used in cameras, phones, and gaming consoles

- Network Attached Storage (NAS) – A mini-server that allows multiple users to store and access files

For long-term storage, external HDDs are cheaper. For speed, external SSDs are better.

RAID: When One Drive Isn't Enough

RAID (Redundant Array of Independent Disks) is a way to use multiple drives for speed, redundancy, or both.

Common RAID Levels:

✓ RAID 0 (Striping) – Splits data across multiple drives for speed, but no redundancy (if one drive fails, all data is lost).

✓ RAID 1 (Mirroring) – Copies data to two drives; if one fails, the other has a backup.

✓ RAID 5 (Striping with Parity) – Balances speed and redundancy, using multiple drives plus a parity drive for backup.

✓ RAID 10 (Striping + Mirroring) – The best of both worlds—fast and redundant, but requires at least 4 drives.

For home users, RAID 1 is best for simple backups. For businesses, RAID 5 or RAID 10 are ideal.

Cloud Storage: The Internet Hard Drive

Cloud storage allows you to store files online, accessible from anywhere.

Popular Cloud Services:

☁ Google Drive – Free 15GB, good for documents and backups

☁ Dropbox – Great for team collaboration and file sharing

☁ OneDrive – Microsoft's cloud storage, integrates with Windows and Office

☁ iCloud – Apple's cloud solution for macOS and iOS users

Pros of Cloud Storage:

✓ Access files anywhere

✓ Automatic backups

✓ Easy file sharing

Cons of Cloud Storage:

✗ Requires internet access

✗ Security concerns (your data is stored on third-party servers).

Best practice? Use both local and cloud storage for redundancy.

Data Backup: Don't Risk Losing Everything

Nothing is worse than losing important files because of a system crash or accidental deletion. That's why regular backups are essential.

The 3-2-1 Backup Rule

✓ 3 copies of your data

✓ 2 different storage types (HDD, SSD, cloud)

✓ 1 copy stored offsite (cloud or external drive in another location)

Backup software like Acronis, Macrium Reflect, or Windows Backup can automate this process.

Quick Check: Test Your Knowledge

1. What's the main difference between an HDD and an SSD?

2. Why is an NVMe SSD faster than a SATA SSD?

3. What is the main advantage of RAID 1?

4. Name two advantages of using cloud storage.

5. What does the 3-2-1 backup rule mean?

Chapter 5

Mobile and Laptop Hardware – Compact Power on the Go

Computers used to be giant machines that filled entire rooms. Now, we carry powerful computing devices in our pockets and backpacks. Laptops and mobile devices have revolutionized how we work, play, and stay connected.

But here's the catch: smaller hardware comes with trade-offs. Laptops and mobile devices are designed for portability, battery efficiency, and compactness, but this often means less power, limited upgradability, and unique troubleshooting challenges.

In this chapter, we'll break down how mobile and laptop hardware differs from desktops, the key components that make them work, and common troubleshooting tips.

Laptops vs. Desktops: The Hardware Trade-Off
While laptops and desktops share similar components, their design priorities are very different.

Feature	Desktop PC	Laptop
Performance	More powerful (high wattage)	Lower power to conserve battery
Portability	No, stays in one place	Yes, designed for mobility
Cooling	Large fans, better airflow	Small fans, less cooling space
Upgradability	Easy (swap RAM, GPU, SSD)	Limited (some parts soldered)
Battery Life	N/A (plugged in)	Runs on battery (varies by model)

Laptops are great for on-the-go productivity, but desktops still dominate in raw power, gaming, and upgradability.

Key Laptop Components

1. Laptop CPUs: Power vs. Efficiency

Laptops use low-power CPUs optimized for battery life and heat management.

✓ Intel Core i5/i7/i9 (U-series, H-series) – Common in business and gaming laptops

✓ AMD Ryzen 5/7/9 (U-series, H-series) – Great performance and efficiency

✓ Apple M1/M2/M3 – Apple's custom ARM-based chips, highly power-efficient.

Unlike desktops, laptop CPUs are usually soldered onto the motherboard, meaning no upgrades after purchase.

2. Laptop GPUs: Integrated vs. Dedicated Graphics

✓ Integrated Graphics (Intel Iris Xe, AMD Radeon, Apple GPU) – Built into the CPU, good for basic tasks

✓ Dedicated GPUs (NVIDIA RTX, AMD Radeon RX) – Separate chips, better for gaming and video editing.

Gaming laptops have high-performance GPUs, but they generate more heat and drain battery faster.

3. Storage: SSDs Are the Norm

Most modern laptops use SSDs (solid-state drives) instead of HDDs because they are faster, quieter, and more power-efficient.

✓ SATA SSDs – Slower but still better than HDDs

✓ NVMe SSDs – Super-fast and compact (found in premium laptops)

Some laptops have removable SSDs, while others use soldered storage, making upgrades impossible.

4. RAM: More is Better (But Not Always Upgradable)

✓ 8GB RAM – Bare minimum for most tasks

✓ 16GB RAM – Ideal for multitasking, creative work

✓ 32GB+ RAM – For professionals, video editing, and gaming.

Many thin laptops now use soldered RAM, meaning no upgrades after purchase.

5. Laptop Batteries: Power on the Go

Laptop batteries use Lithium-Ion (Li-ion) or Lithium-Polymer (Li-Po) cells.

✓ Battery life depends on usage – More powerful hardware drains the battery faster

✓ Charging cycles affect lifespan – Batteries degrade over time, lasting 2-4 years

✓ Fast charging – Many new laptops support quick charging via USB-C.

Pro Tip: To extend battery life, avoid letting it drain to 0% too often and keep it between 20%-80% charge.

Mobile Devices: Hardware in Your Pocket

Smartphones and tablets are built with even smaller, more efficient hardware than laptops.

✓ ARM-based CPUs – Used in smartphones and tablets (Apple A-series, Qualcomm Snapdragon, Samsung Exynos)

✓ Integrated storage – No upgradable SSDs, usually 128GB-1TB internal storage

✓ No fans – Mobile devices rely on passive cooling, meaning they can overheat if overworked

Troubleshooting Common Laptop & Mobile Issues

1. Laptop Won't Turn On

✓ Check the power adapter and battery

✓ Try a hard reset (remove battery, hold power button for 30 sec, reconnect battery)

✓ Test with another charger if available

2. Overheating Issues

✓ Clean out dust from vents and fans

✓ Use a cooling pad to improve airflow

✓ Check Task Manager for high CPU usage

3. Slow Performance

✓ Upgrade RAM or switch to an SSD (if possible)

✓ Disable startup programs in Windows

✓ Keep the OS and drivers updated

4. Battery Draining Too Fast

✓ Lower screen brightness and close unused apps

✓ Use Battery Saver Mode

✓ Check for background apps consuming power

5. Mobile Device Freezing or Crashing

✓ Restart the device

✓ Clear app cache/data

✓ Factory reset (as a last resort)

Quick Check: Test Your Knowledge

1. What's one key difference between laptop and desktop hardware?

2. Why can't you upgrade the CPU on most laptops?

3. What's the advantage of an NVMe SSD over a SATA SSD?

4. What's one way to extend battery life on a laptop?

5. If your laptop is overheating, what's the first thing you should check?

Chapter 6

Operating System Basics – The Software That Runs the Show

Imagine buying a brand-new car, only to realize there's no steering wheel, no dashboard, and no way to control it. That's what a computer would be without an Operating System (OS).

The OS is the middleman between you and your computer's hardware. It manages everything—from running programs to handling files, keeping security in check, and making sure your mouse click actually does something.

In this chapter, we'll cover:

✓ The different types of operating systems (Windows, macOS, Linux, and Mobile OSs)

✓ How to install, upgrade, and configure an OS

✓ Common troubleshooting tips for OS-related issues

Popular Operating Systems and Their Strengths

There's no one-size-fits-all OS. Each system has its strengths and weaknesses, depending on what you need.

1. Windows – The Versatile Powerhouse

✓ Most widely used OS—found in homes, offices, and gaming rigs

✓ User-friendly interface with a Start menu and taskbar

✓ Supports the most software (Microsoft Office, Adobe, games, etc.)

✓ Windows Updates ensure security but can sometimes be annoying

Popular Windows Versions:

- Windows 10 – Still widely used, stable, and supported

- Windows 11 – Modern design, better performance, and enhanced security

- Windows Server – For enterprise-level computing and IT management

✓ Best for: General users, businesses, gamers

✗ Downside: Prone to malware if not properly secured

2. macOS – Apple's Premium Experience

✓ Smooth, polished interface with great stability

✓ Optimized for Apple hardware (MacBooks, iMacs)

✓ Deep integration with iPhones, iPads, and Apple Watches

✓ Excellent built-in security (Gatekeeper, FileVault)

Popular macOS Versions:

- macOS Ventura – Improved multitasking features

- macOS Sonoma (latest) – Performance and UI improvements

Best for: Creative professionals, Apple users

Downside: Expensive hardware, limited gaming options

3. Linux – The Power User's Playground

✓ Free and open-source with various distributions (Ubuntu, Fedora, Kali, etc.)

✓ Highly customizable—from the desktop environment to core system tweaks

✓ More secure than Windows (fewer viruses, better system control)

✓ Lightweight versions available for older computers

Popular Linux Distros:

- Ubuntu – User-friendly, great for beginners

- Kali Linux – Cybersecurity and ethical hacking

- CentOS / RHEL – Used in enterprise environments

✓ Best for: Developers, cybersecurity experts, IT pros

Downside: Steeper learning curve, not all software is supported

4. Mobile Operating Systems

Computers aren't the only devices with an OS— smartphones and tablets have their own systems.

✓ Android – Open-source, used by Samsung, Google Pixel, and others

✓ iOS – Apple's secure and smooth mobile OS

Key Differences:

✓ Android is more customizable (custom ROMs, app sideloading)

✓ iOS is more secure but locked down

✓ Best for: Mobile users, tablets, wearable tech

Downside: Limited customizability (iOS), fragmentation (Android)

Installing and Upgrading an OS

At some point, you'll need to install or upgrade an operating system—whether setting up a new PC, fixing a corrupted OS, or just staying updated.

Step 1: Choosing the Right OS Version

✓ Check hardware compatibility before installing

✓ For Windows users, decide between Windows 10 or 11

✓ For Linux, pick a distro suited for your needs

✓ macOS upgrades are limited to Apple-supported devices

Step 2: Installation Methods

1. Clean Installation (Fresh Start)

✓ Wipes everything and installs the OS from scratch

✓ Best for new systems, fixing major issues, or switching OSs

✓ Requires a bootable USB drive or installation media

2. Upgrade Installation (Keeping Files & Apps)

✓ Keeps personal files and applications

✓ Best when upgrading from an older version of the same OS

✓ Available for Windows and macOS upgrades

3. Virtual Machines (Running Multiple OSs)

✓ Allows running Windows on macOS, or Linux on Windows

✓ Popular VM software:

  - VirtualBox (free, supports multiple OSs)

  - VMware Workstation (premium, better performance)

  - Hyper-V (built into Windows Pro versions)

✓ Best for testing new OSs without fully installing them

Configuring an OS after Installation

Once your OS is installed, it's time to set it up for optimal performance.

✓ Update the OS immediately (Windows Update, macOS Software Update)

✓ Install essential drivers (graphics, chipset, Wi-Fi)

✓ Set up user accounts and security settings

✓ Customize settings (display, power options, default apps)

✓ Install necessary software (browsers, office tools, antivirus)

Troubleshooting Common OS Issues

1. System Won't Boot

✓ Check boot order in BIOS/UEFI

✓ Try Safe Mode (Windows) or Recovery Mode (macOS)

✓ Use a bootable USB to repair the system

2. Slow Performance

✓ Check Task Manager for resource-heavy programs

✓ Disable startup apps that slow down boot time

✓ Free up disk space and defragment the hard drive (if using HDD)

3. Blue Screen of Death (BSOD) on Windows

✓ Run Windows Memory Diagnostic

✓ Check for driver updates

✓ Uninstall recent updates if the issue started after an update

4. macOS Freezing or Not Responding

✓ Force quit unresponsive apps (Command + Option + Esc)

✓ Boot into Safe Mode and check for system issues

✓ Reset NVRAM and SMC (for power and hardware settings)

5. Linux Boot Issues

✓ Reinstall GRUB bootloader (if system won't boot)

✓ Check for kernel updates or compatibility issues

✓ Use Live USB to repair the installation

Quick Check: Test Your Knowledge
1. What are the three main desktop operating systems?

2. Name one advantage and one disadvantage of Linux.

3. What's the difference between a clean installation and an upgrade installation?

4. Why might you use a virtual machine instead of installing an OS directly?

5. If Windows is running slowly, what's one way to improve performance?

Chapter 7

Command Line and System Utilities – Mastering the Hidden Power of Your OS

Most people love pointing and clicking their way through an operating system. It's easy, intuitive, and gets the job done. But here's a secret: the real power of any OS lies in the command line.

Want to fix a system issue when the GUI won't load?

Need to find hidden details about your network or hardware?

Trying to automate tasks like file management?

The command line is faster, more efficient, and often the only way to troubleshoot deep system problems.

In this chapter, we'll cover:

✓ Essential Windows and Linux commands

✓ System utilities for troubleshooting and performance tuning

Windows Command Line (CMD & PowerShell)

Windows provides two powerful command-line tools:

✓ Command Prompt (CMD) – Basic command-line tool for Windows

✓ PowerShell – A more advanced scripting tool for system administration

Let's start with some essential CMD commands every IT pro should know.

Basic Windows Commands

Command	Description
ipconfig	Displays IP address and network info
ping <website>	Checks if a website or IP is reachable
tracert <website>	Shows the route packets take to a destination
tasklist	Lists running processes
taskkill /IM <process>.exe /F	Forces a program to close
chkdsk /f	Checks and fixes disk errors
sfc /scannow	Scans and repairs corrupt system files
netstat -an	Shows network connections
shutdown /r /t 0	Restarts the computer immediately

Example: Checking Network Issues

If your internet is acting up, open CMD and type:

ipconfig /all

This will show IP address, DNS servers, MAC address, and more.

PowerShell: The Advanced Windows Tool

PowerShell is more powerful than CMD because it uses scripts and automation.

Example: Get system information

Get-ComputerInfo

Example: Restart a service (e.g., Wi-Fi)

Restart-Service -Name WLANAutoConfig

Example: Find and uninstall a program

Get-AppxPackage spotify | Remove-AppxPackage

If you're working in IT, learning PowerShell is a must!

Linux Terminal Commands

Linux doesn't have a GUI-based Task Manager or Control Panel, so most troubleshooting is done through the terminal.

Basic Linux Commands

Command	Description
ls	Lists files in a directory
cd <directory>	Changes directories
pwd	Shows current directory
mkdir <folder>	Creates a new folder
rm -rf <folder>	Deletes a folder (be careful!)
cp file1 file2	Copies files
mv file1 file2	Moves or renames files
top	Shows running processes (like Task Manager)
ps aux	Lists all active processes
kill <PID>	Kills a process by Process ID
df -h	Shows disk usage
free -m	Displays memory usage
ifconfig or ip a	Shows network info
ping google.com	Checks network connectivity

Example: Finding a Misbehaving Process

If your Linux system is slow, open the terminal and run:

top

This shows which processes are using the most CPU and RAM.

To stop a process, find its PID and run:

kill <PID>

Troubleshooting with Built-in Tools

Windows Troubleshooting Tools

✓ Task Manager – `Ctrl + Shift + Esc` to check CPU, RAM, and disk usage

✓ Event Viewer – `eventvwr` to see system logs and errors

✓ System Restore – Rolls back to a previous working state

✓ MSConfig – `msconfig` to manage startup programs

✓ Disk Cleanup & Defrag – Helps free up space and optimize performance

✓ Safe Mode – Starts Windows with minimal drivers for troubleshooting

Example: Checking What's Slowing Down Windows

1. Press Ctrl + Shift + Esc to open Task Manager

2. Check CPU, Memory, and Disk usage

3. If something is using too much RAM, right-click and End Task

Linux Troubleshooting Tools

✓ dmesg – Shows hardware-related logs

✓ journalctl -xe – Checks system logs for errors

✓ fsck – Scans and repairs file system errors

✓ systemctl – Manages system services (e.g., `systemctl restart network`)

✓ htop – A better version of `top` for monitoring processes

Example: Restarting a Crashed Network in Linux

If your internet stops working, try:

sudo systemctl restart NetworkManager

Quick Check: Test Your Knowledge

1. What's the difference between Command Prompt and PowerShell?

2. Which command shows running processes in Linux?

3. What tool in Windows helps you monitor CPU and RAM usage?

4. How do you restart the network service in Linux?

5. If a Windows PC won't boot properly, what tool can roll it back to a previous state?

Chapter 8

Virtualization and Cloud Computing – The Future of IT Infrastructure

Imagine if you could run multiple computers inside one physical machine or access your data and applications from anywhere in the world without needing a powerful local device.

That's virtualization and cloud computing in action.

These technologies power modern IT infrastructure, data centers, and even gaming.

If you've used Google Drive, Dropbox, or virtual machines, you've already interacted with them.

In this chapter, we'll cover:

✓ What virtualization is and why it's important

✓ How cloud computing works and why businesses rely on it

✓ The benefits, challenges, and security considerations

What is Virtualization?

Virtualization is the process of creating a virtual version of a computer, operating system, or server that runs on top of a physical machine.

Think of it like running multiple apps on your phone—but instead of apps, you're running entire operating systems.

Types of Virtualization

Type	Description	Example
Desktop Virtualization	Runs multiple OSs on a single computer	Running **Windows and Linux** on one machine
Server Virtualization	One physical server hosts multiple virtual servers	Used in **data centers and cloud hosting**
Network Virtualization	Virtual networks operate independently on shared hardware	**SDN (Software-Defined Networking)**
Storage Virtualization	Combines multiple storage devices into one virtual system	Used in **cloud storage solutions**

Popular Virtualization Software

Software	Platform	Use Case
VMware Workstation	Windows/Linux	Professional virtualization
VirtualBox	Windows/Linux/macOS	Free, open-source virtualization
Hyper-V	Windows	Built-in for Windows Pro/Enterprise
KVM	Linux	Enterprise-grade virtualization

Example: Running Linux on a Windows PC

1. Install VirtualBox

2. Create a new virtual machine (VM)

3. Allocate RAM, CPU, and storage

4. Install Linux (Ubuntu, Kali, etc.) inside the VM

Now, you have Windows and Linux running on the same machine—without needing dual boot!

What is Cloud Computing?

Cloud computing allows you to access computing resources (storage, processing, networking) over the internet instead of relying on local hardware.

✓ No need for powerful computers—the cloud handles the heavy lifting

✓ Access your files and applications from anywhere

✓ Easily scale resources up or down

Types of Cloud Computing Services

Service	Description	Example
IaaS (Infrastructure as a Service)	Virtual machines, storage, and networking	**AWS EC2, Google Compute Engine**
PaaS (Platform as a Service)	Tools for developers to build applications	**Google App Engine, Microsoft Azure App Services**
SaaS (Software as a Service)	Software hosted in the cloud	**Google Docs, Dropbox, Microsoft 365**

Example: Using Google Drive (SaaS)

1. Upload a file to Google Drive

2. Access it from any device, anywhere

3. No need for USB drives or external storage

Cloud Deployment Models

Model	Description	Example
Public Cloud	Services offered over the internet to multiple users	**AWS, Google Cloud, Microsoft Azure**
Private Cloud	Cloud infrastructure dedicated to one organization	Used by **banks, government agencies**
Hybrid Cloud	Mix of public and private cloud services	Used in **large enterprises**

Example: A Bank's Cloud Strategy

- Uses a private cloud for sensitive customer data

- Uses public cloud (AWS) for general applications

- Combines both in a hybrid model

Benefits of Virtualization and Cloud Computing

✓ Cost Savings – No need to buy expensive hardware

✓ Scalability – Quickly adjust resources based on demand

✓ Disaster Recovery – Data is backed up in multiple locations

✓ Remote Access – Work from anywhere with internet access

✓ Efficient IT Management – Easy deployment of updates and patches

Security Challenges and Considerations

✓ Data Privacy – Who controls your data?

✓ Compliance Issues – Certain industries require strict data handling

✓ Cybersecurity Risks – Cloud servers can be targeted by hackers

✓ Reliability – If the cloud provider goes down, so do your services

Best Practices for Cloud Security

✓ Use strong authentication (MFA)

✓ Encrypt sensitive data

✓ Regularly back up important files

✓ Choose reliable cloud providers

Quick Check: Test Your Knowledge

1. What is virtualization, and why is it useful?

2. Name three types of virtualization and their use cases.

3. What are the three main types of cloud computing services?

4. Give an example of a SaaS application you've used.

5. What's a key security risk of cloud computing, and how can you mitigate it?

Chapter 9

Networking Basics – How Computers Talk to Each Other

Every time you send an email, browse the web, or stream a video, your device is communicating with other computers across a network.

Ever wondered how Wi-Fi works?

Why do some websites load faster than others?

What happens when you type a web address in your browser?

Networking is the backbone of modern computing, and understanding it will make you a better IT professional.

In this chapter, we'll cover:

✓ Different types of networks (LAN, WAN, etc.)

✓ IP addressing (IPv4 vs. IPv6), DHCP, and DNS

Types of Networks

Not all networks are the same. Some connect a few devices in a small office, while others span the entire planet.

1. Local Area Network (LAN)

✓ Covers a small area (home, office, school)

✓ Uses Ethernet cables or Wi-Fi

Examples: Your home Wi-Fi, office network

Why LANs matter:

✓ Faster speeds (Gigabit Ethernet, Wi-Fi 6)

✓ More secure than public networks

✓ Devices can share printers, files, and internet connections

2. Wide Area Network (WAN)

✓ Covers a large area (cities, countries, the world)

✓ Uses fiber optics, satellites, cellular networks

Examples: The Internet, corporate networks spanning multiple offices

Why WANs matter:

✓ Allows companies to connect offices worldwide

✓ Provides remote access to resources

✓ Can be expensive and require advanced security

3. Other Network Types

Network Type	Description	Example
PAN (Personal Area Network)	Very short-range, for personal devices	Bluetooth connections
MAN (Metropolitan Area Network)	Covers a city or large campus	City-wide Wi-Fi networks
SAN (Storage Area Network)	High-speed network for storage	Used in **data centers**

Example: How Your Home Network Works

1. Your ISP (Internet Service Provider) connects your house to the WAN (Internet).

2. Your router creates a LAN for all your devices.

3. Your laptop connects via Wi-Fi or Ethernet.

4. When you type a website, your router sends a request through the WAN to a web server.

IP Addresses: The Internet's Phone Numbers

Every device on a network needs an IP address to communicate.

Think of an IP address like your home address—it tells the network where to send data.

IPv4: The Old Standard

✓ Uses four sets of numbers (e.g., `192.168.1.1`)

✓ Supports ~4.3 billion unique addresses

✓ We are running out of IPv4 addresses

Example: Finding Your IPv4 Address (Windows)

1. Open Command Prompt (`cmd`).

2. Type:

   ipconfig

3. Look for IPv4 Address (e.g., `192.168.1.10`).

IPv6: The Future of Networking

✓ Uses longer addresses (e.g., `2001:db8::ff00:42:8329`)

✓ Supports trillions of devices

✓ More secure and efficient than IPv4

Example: Why IPv6 is Needed

- More people are using smartphones, smart TVs, and IoT devices.

- IPv4 can't provide enough addresses, but IPv6 can.

How Devices Get IP Addresses (DHCP)

When you connect to Wi-Fi, do you manually type an IP address?

No! DHCP (Dynamic Host Configuration Protocol) assigns it automatically.

How DHCP Works:

1. You connect to a Wi-Fi network.

2. The router (DHCP server) assigns your device an IP address.

3. When you disconnect, the IP can be reused for another device.

Example: Why DHCP is Useful

- You don't have to manually configure every device.

- Makes it easy for ISPs to manage millions of users.

DNS: The Internet's Phonebook

When you type www.google.com, your computer doesn't understand names—it understands IP addresses.

DNS (Domain Name System) translates domain names into IP addresses.

Example: How DNS Works

1. You type `www.google.com` into your browser.

2. Your computer asks a DNS server for the IP address.

3. The DNS server responds: `142.250.190.46`

4. Your browser connects to Google's web server.

Example: Checking Your DNS Settings (Windows)

1. Open Command Prompt (`cmd`).

2. Type:

   nslookup google.com

3. You'll see Google's IP address.

Why DNS is Important:

- Without DNS, you'd have to memorize IP addresses!

- DNS makes the internet user-friendly.

Quick Check: Test Your Knowledge

1. What's the difference between a LAN and a WAN?

2. How does DHCP help assign IP addresses?

3. What's the main difference between IPv4 and IPv6?

4. What does DNS do?

5. What command do you use to find your IP address on Windows?

Chapter 10

Network Hardware and Topologies – The Blueprint of Connectivity

I magine trying to build a city without roads, highways, or traffic signals. That's what a network would be like without proper hardware and topology.

Ever wondered what a router actually does?

Why do we need switches, firewalls, and modems?

What's the difference between a star and mesh network?

In this chapter, we'll cover:

✓ Essential networking devices (routers, switches, modems, and firewalls)

✓ Common network topologies (how devices are connected)

Understanding Network Hardware
1. Router – The Traffic Director

A router connects different networks together—most commonly, your home or office network (LAN) to the internet (WAN).

Think of a router as a traffic cop directing data where it needs to go.

Routers assign IP addresses and manage network traffic.

Example: How Your Home Router Works

1. Your internet service provider (ISP) provides internet access.

2. Your router distributes the connection to multiple devices.

3. When you open a website, your router forwards your request to the internet and sends the response back to you.

Common Router Features:

- Wi-Fi broadcasting for wireless connections

- Firewall capabilities for basic security

- Port forwarding to allow external access to internal devices

2. Switch – The Data Distributor

A switch is used in wired networks to connect multiple devices within a LAN (Local Area Network).

Think of a switch as a mail sorter—it efficiently sends data only to the intended recipient.

Example: Why Businesses Use Switches

- Unlike routers, switches don't assign IP addresses—they focus on MAC addresses (hardware identifiers).

- They allow multiple computers to communicate at high speeds.

- They're used in offices, data centers, and large networks.

Types of Switches:

Switch Type	Function
Unmanaged	Simple plug-and-play, no configuration needed
Managed	Can be customized and controlled remotely
PoE (Power over Ethernet)	Powers devices like security cameras through Ethernet cables

3. Modem – The Internet Translator

A modem converts signals between your ISP and your home network.

Think of a modem as a translator between digital (your computer) and analog (internet signals).

Most modern ISPs provide a combo device (modem + router in one).

Types of Modems:

Modem Type	Function
DSL Modem	Connects through telephone lines
Cable Modem	Uses coaxial cables (faster than DSL)
Fiber Modem (ONT)	Converts fiber-optic signals into usable internet

4. Firewall – The Security Guard

A firewall monitors and controls incoming and outgoing network traffic.

Think of it as a bouncer at a nightclub—it only lets in authorized guests.

It can be hardware-based (physical device) or software-based (built into Windows/Linux).

Example: How Firewalls Protect Your Network

1. You try to visit a website.

2. The firewall checks if the site is safe or blacklisted.

3. If the site is safe, it allows traffic through.

4. If it's suspicious, the firewall blocks the request.

Why Firewalls Matter:

- Blocks hackers and malware from entering your network.

- Prevents unauthorized access to sensitive data.

- Used in home, business, and government networks.

Understanding Network Topologies

A network topology describes how devices are physically or logically connected.

Think of it as a city map—how roads (network cables) connect buildings (devices).

Choosing the right topology affects speed, reliability, and scalability.

1. Bus Topology – The Single Highway

Devices share one main cable (bus) to communicate.

Pros: Simple and cheap to set up.

Cons: If the main cable fails, the entire network goes down.

Example: Used in small offices and legacy systems.

2. Star Topology – The Hub and Spoke Model

Devices connect to a central switch or router (like spokes on a wheel).

Pros: If one device fails, the rest of the network stays online.

Cons: If the central device fails, the whole network is down.

Example: Common in home and office networks.

3. Ring Topology – The Circular Highway

Devices are connected in a loop (ring) where data travels in one direction.

Pros: Predictable data flow and no collisions.

Cons: If one device fails, the entire network breaks.

Example: Used in older telecom and industrial networks.

4. Mesh Topology – The Redundancy King

Every device connects to multiple other devices, creating multiple paths.

 Pros: High reliability—if one link fails, data finds another route.

Cons: Expensive and complex to set up.

Example: Used in military, enterprise, and smart city networks.

Comparison of Network Topologies

Topology	Pros	Cons	Example Use Case
Bus	Simple, cheap	Single point of failure	Small networks
Star	Reliable, scalable	Central device is critical	Home & office networks
Ring	Efficient data flow	Failure disrupts the network	Telecom networks
Mesh	Highly fault-tolerant	Expensive, complex	Large-scale enterprises

Quick Check: Test Your Knowledge

1. What's the main job of a router?

2. How does a switch differ from a router?

3. What's the purpose of a modem in a home network?

4. What does a firewall do to protect a network?

5. Which network topology is most reliable but also expensive?

Chapter 11

Wireless Technologies and Security – Cutting the Cords, Keeping It Safe

Gone are the days of tripping over Ethernet cables—wireless technology has taken over!

Ever wondered why some Wi-Fi connections are faster than others?   Why does your connection drop in certain areas of your house? What's the best way to protect your Wi-Fi from hackers?

In this chapter, we'll break down:

✓ Wi-Fi standards and how they've evolved

✓ Wi-Fi security and encryption methods

✓ Troubleshooting common wireless connectivity issues

Wi-Fi Standards: Understanding the Alphabet Soup

Not all Wi-Fi networks are created equal. The Wi-Fi standard (IEEE 802.11) has gone through several upgrades over the years.

Think of it like car models—a 2024 sports car is way faster than a 1999 sedan!

Wi-Fi Standard	Maximum Speed	Frequency	Range	Common Use Case
802.11b (1999)	11 Mbps	2.4 GHz	~150 ft	Early Wi-Fi networks
802.11g (2003)	54 Mbps	2.4 GHz	~150 ft	Upgraded home Wi-Fi
802.11n (2009)	600 Mbps	2.4 & 5 GHz	~300 ft	Modern home Wi-Fi
802.11ac (2013)	1 Gbps+	5 GHz	~300 ft	High-speed streaming, gaming
802.11ax (Wi-Fi 6, 2019)	9.6 Gbps	2.4 & 5 GHz	~500 ft	Smart homes, IoT, 4K/8K streaming

Example: Why Wi-Fi 6 Matters

- More devices can connect without slowing down.

- Uses OFDMA technology to improve efficiency.

- Better range and battery life for mobile devices.

Wi-Fi Frequencies: 2.4 GHz vs. 5 GHz vs. 6 GHz

2.4 GHz:

- Longer range, but slower speeds

- More interference from microwaves, Bluetooth, and neighbors' Wi-Fi

5 GHz:

- Faster speeds, but shorter range

- Less interference, great for streaming and gaming

6 GHz (Wi-Fi 6E):

- Fastest speeds, lowest congestion

- Works best in modern routers and devices

Example: Choosing the Right Frequency

Use Case	Best Frequency

Browsing & emails	2.4 GHz
Gaming & streaming	5 GHz
Future-proofing	6 GHz

Wi-Fi Security: Keeping Hackers Out

✓ Did you know?

An unsecured Wi-Fi network is like leaving your front door wide open—anyone can access it!

1. Wi-Fi Encryption Types

✓ WEP (Wired Equivalent Privacy) – DO NOT USE! It's outdated and easy to hack.

✓ WPA (Wi-Fi Protected Access) – Better than WEP, but still weak.

✓ WPA2 (Wi-Fi Protected Access 2) – Still widely used, but can be hacked with brute force.

✓ WPA3 (Wi-Fi Protected Access 3) – Most secure option, encrypts data better.

Example: Why WPA3 is Better

- Uses stronger encryption (SAE instead of PSK).

- Prevents brute force attacks.

- Even if someone gets your Wi-Fi password, they can't decrypt past data.

Best Practice: Always use WPA2 or WPA3 for security.

2. How to Secure Your Wi-Fi Network

1. Change the Default Router Login

- Many routers come with default usernames and passwords.

- Hackers can easily look these up online.

2. Use a Strong Wi-Fi Password

- Avoid passwords like "password123" or "WiFiHome."

- Use a mix of uppercase, lowercase, numbers, and symbols.

3. Disable WPS (Wi-Fi Protected Setup)

- WPS makes it easier for hackers to guess your PIN.

4. Set Up a Guest Network

- Keep your main devices private by using a separate network for visitors.

5. Update Router Firmware Regularly

- Manufacturers release security patches to fix vulnerabilities.

Example: How to Update Your Router Firmware

1. Log into your router's admin panel (`192.168.1.1` or `192.168.0.1`).

2. Look for a Firmware Update section.

3. Download and install the latest version.

Troubleshooting Common Wi-Fi Issues

Ever had Wi-Fi disconnect for no reason?   Does your signal weaken in certain rooms?   Are you experiencing slow speeds?

1. Slow Wi-Fi Speed

✓ Possible Causes:

- Too many devices slowing the network

- Interference from microwaves, Bluetooth, or other Wi-Fi networks

- ISP throttling or network congestion

✓ Solutions:

- Use 5 GHz or 6 GHz instead of 2.4 GHz.

- Place the router in a central location, away from walls.

- Restart your router and limit background downloads.

2. Weak Wi-Fi Signal

✓ Possible Causes:

- Router is too far from your device.

- Physical barriers like walls and furniture.

✓ Solutions:

- Use a Wi-Fi extender or mesh system.

- Upgrade to a router with stronger antennas.

3. Wi-Fi Keeps Disconnecting

✓ Possible Causes:

- Too many devices on the network.

- Outdated router firmware.

- ISP issues.

✓ Solutions:

- Restart the router and update the firmware.

- Limit the number of connected devices.

Example: Checking Wi-Fi Signal Strength (Windows)

1. Open Command Prompt (`cmd`).

2. Type:

   netsh wlan show interfaces

3. Look for Signal Strength (percentage).

- Above 80% = Excellent

- 50-79% = Good

- Below 50% = Weak signal

Quick Check: Test Your Knowledge

1. What's the difference between 2.4 GHz, 5 GHz, and 6 GHz Wi-Fi?

2. What's the most secure Wi-Fi encryption method?

3. Why should you disable WPS on your router?

4. What's one way to boost your Wi-Fi signal?

5. How do you check Wi-Fi signal strength in Windows?

Chapter 12

Cybersecurity Essentials – Defending the Digital Frontier

Imagine leaving your front door wide open in a busy city—anyone could walk in. That's exactly what happens when you ignore cybersecurity in the digital world.

Every day, millions of cyberattacks target individuals and businesses. Hackers steal data, deploy viruses, and cause billions in damages. But you don't have to be a victim—understanding cybersecurity can keep you safe!

In this chapter, we'll cover:

✓ Types of cyber threats and how they work

✓ Best practices for protection

✓ Firewalls, antivirus software, and encryption

Understanding Cyber Threats

Hackers have plenty of tricks to compromise your system. Let's break down the most common types of cyber threats.

1. Malware – The Digital Parasite

Malware (short for "malicious software") infects devices and causes damage. It can steal data, spy on users, or destroy files.

Common Types of Malware:

Type	What It Does	Example
Virus	Attaches to files and spreads when opened	Infected email attachments
Worm	Spreads without user action	Self-replicating network attack
Trojan	Disguises as a legitimate file but contains malware	Fake software downloads
Ransomware	Encrypts files and demands payment for access	WannaCry attack
Spyware	Secretly collects user data	Keyloggers, tracking software
Adware	Displays unwanted ads and slows devices	Pop-up ads, browser hijackers

Example: How Ransomware Works

1. You download an email attachment from an unknown sender.

2. The ransomware encrypts all your files, locking you out.

3. A message appears: "Pay $500 in Bitcoin to unlock your files."

4. Even if you pay, there's no guarantee you'll get your files back.

How to Protect Yourself:

✓ Never open suspicious attachments.

✓ Back up important files regularly.

✓ Use strong security software to detect threats.

2. Phishing – The Digital Con Game

Phishing is a cyberattack where hackers trick users into revealing sensitive information. Often involves fake emails, messages, or websites that look legitimate.

Example: How Phishing Works

1. You receive an email from "Your Bank" asking you to reset your password.

2. The email contains a link to a fake website that looks real.

3. You enter your username and password.

4. The hacker now has access to your bank account.

How to Spot Phishing Emails:

✓ Check the sender's email address. (Legit companies don't use random Gmail accounts.)

✓ Hover over links before clicking. (Fake sites often have misspelled URLs.)

✓ Look for spelling errors and urgent language. (Hackers rush you into making mistakes.)

3. Denial-of-Service (DoS) Attacks – Crashing the Party

DoS and DDoS attacks flood a website with fake traffic, causing it to crash. Used to disrupt businesses, gaming servers, or government websites.

How DoS Attacks Work?

1. A hacker overloads a server with too many requests.

2. Legitimate users can't access the site.

3. The attack continues until the site is fixed or protected.

Example: DDoS Attack on PlayStation Network (2014)

Hackers flooded Sony's servers, crashing online gaming services for days.

How to Prevent DoS Attacks:

✓ Use firewalls to filter traffic.

✓ Enable DDoS protection on your website or network.

✓ Monitor for unusual spikes in traffic.

2. Cybersecurity Protection Methods

Now that we know the threats, let's talk about defensive strategies.

1. Firewalls – The Digital Gatekeeper

A firewall monitors and controls incoming and outgoing traffic. Acts like a security guard, blocking unauthorized access.

Types of Firewalls:

Firewall Type	Function
Hardware Firewall	Physical device between your network and the internet
Software Firewall	Built into Windows/macOS, monitors app traffic
Cloud Firewall	Filters traffic in cloud environments (AWS, Azure)

Best Practice: Always enable firewalls on routers and computers.

2. Antivirus and Anti-Malware Software

Antivirus software detects and removes malware before it causes damage.

Popular Antivirus Programs:

- Windows Defender (built into Windows)

- Bitdefender

- Malwarebytes

- Norton

Best Practice:

- Keep your antivirus updated to detect new threats.

- Run regular system scans for hidden malware.

3. **Encryption – Locking Up Your Data**

Encryption converts data into unreadable code that only authorized users can access. Used to protect emails, files, and passwords.

Common Encryption Methods:

Encryption Type	Use Case
AES (Advanced Encryption Standard)	Protects sensitive data (banking, passwords)
TLS/SSL	Secures websites (HTTPS)
BitLocker	Encrypts entire hard drives (Windows)

Example: How Encryption Protects Your Data

1. You send an encrypted email with AES-256.

2. Even if a hacker intercepts it, they can't read the contents without the encryption key.

Best Practice:

- Always use HTTPS websites (look for the padlock icon).

- Encrypt sensitive files before storing them in the cloud.

Quick Check: Test Your Knowledge

1. What's the difference between a virus, worm, and Trojan?

2. How can you identify a phishing email?

3. What does a firewall do?

4. Why is encryption important for security?

5. Name one way to prevent malware infections.

Chapter 13

User Access and Authentication – Locking the Digital Doors

Imagine if anyone could walk into your house, take your belongings, and leave without consequences. That's what happens in the digital world when access controls are weak.

Every year, millions of passwords get stolen due to poor security practices. Cybercriminals use social engineering and phishing to trick users into giving up access. Without proper authentication, data breaches and identity theft skyrocket.

In this chapter, we'll cover:

✓ How passwords and authentication work

✓ Multi-Factor Authentication (MFA) and why you need it

✓ How hackers trick users with social engineering

✓ Best practices for securing accounts

Password Security – The First Line of Defense

Passwords are the keys to your digital life. But most people:

✘ Use weak passwords like "password123"

✘ Reuse the same password across multiple sites

✘ Forget to change passwords after a breach

Fact: Over 80% of hacking-related breaches are due to weak or stolen passwords.

Creating a Strong Password

A good password should be:

✓ At least 12–16 characters long

✓ A mix of uppercase, lowercase, numbers, and symbols

✓ Not a common phrase or dictionary word

Example of Weak vs. Strong Passwords:

Weak Password	Strong Password
12345678	fT9#xRk8!qP2&
password	M0nkey$@Tree#77
letmein	Gr3@tW@ll_99!

Best Practices:

- Never write down your passwords or store them in plain text.

- Use a passphrase (a random sentence) instead of just a word.

- Enable password managers to generate and store complex passwords securely.

Multi-Factor Authentication (MFA) – Extra Security for Your Accounts

Passwords alone aren't enough—if a hacker steals your password, they can log in as you. MFA adds an extra layer of security.

MFA requires two or more of the following:

- Something you know (password, PIN)
- Something you have (phone, security key)
- Something you are (fingerprint, face scan)

Example of MFA in Action:

1. You enter your password on a banking website.

2. The website sends a one-time code to your phone.

3. You enter the code to confirm your identity.

Best Practice:

- Enable MFA on email, social media, banking, and work accounts.

- Use authentication apps like Google Authenticator or Microsoft Authenticator.

- Avoid using SMS-based MFA if possible (SIM swapping attacks exist).

Access Control – Limiting Who Can Do What

✓ Access control determines who gets access to what.

✓ Companies use it to protect sensitive files and systems.

Types of Access Control

Type	How It Works	Example
Role-Based Access Control (RBAC)	Access depends on job role	Only HR can access payroll data
Mandatory Access Control (MAC)	Strict access rules set by administrators	Military and government systems
Discretionary Access Control (DAC)	Users control their own file permissions	Personal file-sharing settings

Example: How RBAC Works in a Company

- A junior employee can view documents but can't edit or delete them.

- An IT admin has full access to change security settings.

Best Practice:

- Use least privilege access—give users only the access they need.

- Review access permissions regularly to prevent security risks.

Social Engineering – When Hackers Manipulate Humans

Cybercriminals don't just hack computers—they hack people. Social engineering attacks trick users into giving up passwords, data, or access.

Common Social Engineering Attacks

Attack Type	How It Works	Example
Phishing	Fake emails trick users into revealing info	"Your bank account is locked! Click here to reset your password."
Vishing (Voice Phishing)	Attackers call pretending to be a trusted source	"Hi, this is IT Support. I need your login to fix your account."
Smishing (SMS Phishing)	Fake text messages lure users into scams	"Amazon: Your package is delayed. Click this link to reschedule."
Baiting	Attackers leave infected USB drives for users to plug in	A USB labeled "Confidential Salary Data" left in a parking lot
Pretexting	Criminals impersonate authority figures to gain trust	"This is the IRS. We need your Social Security number."

Example: How Phishing Works

1. You receive an email from "PayPal" saying there's an issue with your account.

2. The email contains a fake link to a PayPal login page.

3. You enter your username and password.

4. The hacker steals your credentials and logs into your real account.

Best Practices for Protecting Against Attacks

1. Always verify requests for sensitive information.

2. Never click on suspicious links in emails or messages.

3. Check the sender's email address carefully.

4. Enable MFA on all important accounts.

5. Keep software and security updates installed.

6. Use strong, unique passwords for each account.

Example: Checking for Phishing Emails

✅ Real PayPal Email: `support@paypal.com`

❌ Fake PayPal Email: `support@pay-pal.com`

Tip: Hover over links before clicking! Fake links might lead to:

❌ `www.paypal-security-check.com` (Fake)

✅ `www.paypal.com` (Real)

Quick Check: Test Your Knowledge

1. What makes a strong password?

2. Why is multi-factor authentication important?

3. What's the difference between RBAC, MAC, and DAC?

4. Name one type of social engineering attack.

5. How can you identify a phishing email?

Chapter 14

Hardware and Software Troubleshooting – Fixing Tech like a Pro

E ver had a computer that refused to turn on, crashed randomly, or just ran painfully slow?

Maybe your Wi-Fi keeps disconnecting, or your printer has decided it no longer wants to print.

Every tech professional needs troubleshooting skills. Understanding how to diagnose and fix problems saves time, money, and frustration. Whether it's a PC, laptop, or mobile device, knowing the right tools and methods is key.

In this chapter, we'll cover:

✓ Common hardware and software problems

✓ Step-by-step troubleshooting techniques

✓ Using system logs and diagnostic tools

The Golden Rules of Troubleshooting

Before we jump into specific problems, here are five golden rules every troubleshooter should follow:

1. Start with the basics – Is it plugged in? Is it turned on? Is the battery charged?

2. Identify the symptoms – What exactly is happening? Error messages? Slow performance?

3. Recreate the problem – Can you make the issue happen again? (This helps isolate the cause.)

4. Rule out causes systematically – Try one fix at a time to see what works.

5. Document the steps taken – If you can't fix it, your notes will help the next technician.

Common Hardware Problems and Fixes

Computers and laptops have several hardware components that can fail. Let's break down common hardware issues and how to fix them.

1. PC Won't Power On

Possible Causes:

- Loose power cable or dead battery

- Faulty power supply unit (PSU)

- Bad motherboard or RAM

Troubleshooting Steps:

1. Check power connections – Ensure everything is plugged in properly.

2. Try a different power outlet or power adapter.

3. Remove the battery (laptops only) and plug in the AC adapter.

4. Listen for beeps – Some motherboards give beep codes that indicate errors.

5. Swap out RAM – Faulty RAM can prevent booting.

2. Overheating and Unexpected Shutdowns

Possible Causes:

- Dust blocking airflow

- Faulty cooling fan or dried thermal paste

- Overclocking causing excessive heat

Troubleshooting Steps:

1. Check for dust buildup inside the case and clean it.

2. Ensure fans are spinning properly and replace them if needed.

3. Apply new thermal paste to the CPU.

4. Use system monitoring tools like HWMonitor to check temperatures.

3. No Display or Distorted Graphics

Possible Causes:

- Faulty GPU (graphics card)

- Loose monitor cable

- Corrupted graphics driver

Troubleshooting Steps:

1. Check connections – Ensure the monitor cable is secure.

2. Try another monitor or use a different display cable.

3. Update or reinstall graphics drivers.

4. If using a dedicated GPU, switch to onboard graphics to see if the issue persists.

4. Keyboard and Mouse Not Responding

Possible Causes:

- Loose USB connections

- Driver issues

- Wireless interference (for Bluetooth devices)

Troubleshooting Steps:

1. Unplug and reconnect the device (try different USB ports).

2. Restart the computer and check if the issue persists.

3. Reinstall keyboard/mouse drivers in Device Manager.

4. Replace the batteries if using a wireless device.

Common Software Problems and Fixes

1. Slow Performance or Freezing

Possible Causes:

- Too many background apps running

- Low disk space

- Corrupt system files

Troubleshooting Steps:

1. Close unnecessary programs in Task Manager (Ctrl + Shift + Esc).

2. Run "Disk Cleanup" to free up space.

3. Check for updates (Windows/macOS updates may fix bugs).

4. Run "sfc /scannow" in Command Prompt to check for system file errors.

2. Blue Screen of Death (BSOD) – Windows Crash

Possible Causes:

- Faulty hardware (RAM, hard drive, GPU)

- Corrupt drivers or system files

Troubleshooting Steps:

1. Write down the error code displayed on the blue screen.

2. Boot into Safe Mode (press F8 or Shift + Restart on Windows 10/11).

3. Update or roll back drivers using Device Manager.

4. Run Windows Memory Diagnostic to check for RAM issues.

5. Check hard drive health using chkdsk /f.

3. Applications Crashing or Not Opening

Possible Causes:

- Corrupt installation files

- Compatibility issues

- Insufficient system resources

Troubleshooting Steps:

1. Restart the computer and try opening the app again.

2. Check for software updates – New versions fix bugs.

3. Run the program as an administrator (Right-click > "Run as Administrator").

4. Reinstall the application.

System Logs and Diagnostic Tools – Finding the Root Cause

Logs and diagnostic tools help track errors and system health.

1. Windows Event Viewer – Logging System Issues

How to Open It:

- Press Win + R, type eventvwr, and press Enter.

- Look under Windows Logs > System to check for errors.

Useful for diagnosing crashes, driver failures, and security issues.

2. Task Manager – Monitoring System Performance

How to Open It:

- Press Ctrl + Shift + Esc.

✓ Check for high CPU, RAM, or disk usage.

✓ End unresponsive programs manually.

3. Command Line Diagnostics

Command	Function
ipconfig /all	Displays network configuration
sfc /scannow	Scans and repairs corrupt system files
chkdsk /f	Scans and fixes hard drive errors
ping (website)	Checks network connectivity

Example:

To check if a website is reachable, type:

ping google.com

If you get replies, the connection is working!

Quick Check: Test Your Troubleshooting Knowledge

1. What should you check first if a PC won't turn on?

2. What tool allows you to view system error logs?

3. What is the most common cause of overheating in computers?

4. What command scans and repairs Windows system files?

5. How can you check if a network connection is working?

Chapter 15

Preventive Maintenance and Best Practices – Keeping IT Running Smoothly

Imagine buying a brand-new car but never changing the oil, never checking the tires, and ignoring the warning lights. How long would it last?

Now apply that logic to your computer hardware and software. Dust, overheating, and outdated software are like rust on a car. Without proper maintenance, systems slow down, crash, or fail completely. Data loss happens when backups don't exist.

The goal of this chapter:

✓ Keep your PCs, laptops, and mobile devices running efficiently.

✓ Avoid unnecessary repairs and downtime.

✓ Learn backup and recovery best practices so you never lose critical data.

Routine Maintenance – The Key to Longevity

✓ Regular maintenance prevents major failures.

✓ IT professionals follow scheduled checkups to ensure everything runs smoothly.

1. Cleaning and Dust Management

Over time, dust builds up inside a computer, clogging fans and causing overheating.

Best Practices for Cleaning:

✓ Use compressed air to remove dust from fans and vents.

✓ Clean keyboards with isopropyl alcohol to remove grime.

✓ Keep liquids away from laptops and desktops to prevent spills.

✓ Store computers in cool, dry places to avoid humidity damage.

Pro Tip:

- If a PC is running hotter than normal, check for dust buildup inside!

2. Software Updates – The Security Lifeline

Outdated software is the 1 reason for security vulnerabilities. Cybercriminals exploit old versions of Windows, macOS, and applications.

What Needs Updating?

✅ Operating System (Windows, macOS, Linux)

✅ Antivirus & security software

✅ Web browsers and plugins (Chrome, Firefox, Edge, etc.)

✅ Device drivers (Graphics card, Wi-Fi, Printer, etc.)

Best Practice:

- Enable automatic updates wherever possible.

- Regularly check for updates in Windows Update or Software Update (Mac).

How to Manually Update Windows:

1. Click Start > Settings > Windows Update.

2. Click Check for Updates and install available updates.

How to Manually Update macOS:

1. Open System Preferences > Software Update.

2. Click Update Now if an update is available.

Pro Tip:

- Restart your system after updates to ensure all changes apply correctly!

Hardware Maintenance – Extending Device Lifespan

Every hardware component has a lifespan. Preventive maintenance helps reduce wear and tear.

1. Hard Drive Health Checks

Hard drives can fail unexpectedly, leading to data loss.

Best Practices for Hard Drives:

✓ Run disk cleanup regularly to remove unnecessary files.

✓ Check for errors using built-in tools (e.g., `chkdsk` on Windows, Disk Utility on macOS).

✓ Defragment HDDs (not SSDs!) to optimize performance.

How to Check Hard Drive Health on Windows:

1. Open Command Prompt and type:

  chkdsk /f

2. Restart the computer to scan and fix disk errors.

Pro Tip:

- SSDs don't need defragmentation! They wear out faster if defragged.

2. Battery Maintenance for Laptops and Mobile Devices

Laptop and phone batteries degrade over time. The average lithium-ion battery lasts 2-3 years before performance drops.

Best Practices for Longer Battery Life:

✅ Don't leave devices plugged in 24/7 – it reduces battery lifespan.

✅ Charge between 20-80% instead of 0-100%.

✅ Enable battery-saving modes to reduce power consumption.

✅ Store batteries in cool places – heat shortens lifespan.

Pro Tip:

- Avoid fast charging unless necessary. It generates heat, which degrades the battery faster.

Backup and Recovery Planning – Preparing for the Worst

What if your hard drive crashes today? Would you lose everything? IT professionals always plan for data recovery.

1. The 3-2-1 Backup Rule

The gold standard for data protection:

3 – Keep three copies of your data.

2 – Store backups on two different types of media (e.g., external drive + cloud).

1 – Keep one backup offsite (cloud or another location).

Best Backup Options:

✓ External Hard Drives – Good for quick local backups.

✓ Cloud Storage (Google Drive, OneDrive, iCloud) – Remote access, automatic sync.

✓ Network Attached Storage (NAS) – Local network backups for businesses.

Pro Tip:

- Schedule automatic backups to avoid forgetting!

2. How to Back Up Data on Windows & macOS

Windows Backup (File History & System Image)

1. Go to Settings > Update & Security > Backup.

2. Select Backup using File History and choose an external drive.

Mac Backup (Time Machine)

1. Open System Preferences > Time Machine.

2. Select Backup Disk and choose an external drive.

Cloud Backup Services (For Extra Protection):

✅ Google Drive (15GB free)

✅ OneDrive (5GB free)

✅ Dropbox (2GB free)

Pro Tip:

- Test your backups regularly to ensure they work!

3. Disaster Recovery – What to Do When Things Go Wrong

If your system fails completely, you need a recovery plan.

Common Recovery Options:

✅ System Restore – Rolls Windows back to an earlier point.

✅ Recovery Drive/USB – Boot from a recovery disk to fix startup issues.

✅ Cloud Recovery (Windows 11/macOS) – Reinstall OS directly from the internet.

Pro Tip:

- Keep a bootable USB drive with system recovery tools handy.

Quick Check: Test Your Knowledge

1. What is the 3-2-1 backup rule?

2. How often should you clean dust from your PC?

3. Why is it important to update software regularly?

4. What is the best way to extend battery lifespan?

5. Name one tool used to check hard drive health.

Chapter 16

IT Ethics and Customer Service – The Human Side of Tech

Being a great IT professional isn't just about fixing computers—it's about helping people and maintaining ethical standards.

Ever dealt with an impatient or frustrated customer? Have you ever had access to sensitive information that needed confidentiality? Would you know what to do if asked to "bend the rules" on data security?

In this chapter, we'll cover:

✓ How to communicate effectively with users.

✓ The best customer service practices in IT.

✓ Ethical dilemmas and how to handle them.

Customer Service in IT – Handling People Like a Pro

IT professionals often work directly with customers, employees, or end-users. A good attitude and clear communication make all the difference.

1. The Basics of Effective IT Communication

Golden Rule: Speak in a way the user understands. Avoid technical jargon unless necessary.

Scenario: A customer calls saying, "My computer is broken!"

Bad response: "Have you checked your BIOS settings to ensure your firmware isn't interfering with POST?"

Good response: "Can you tell me exactly what happens when you try to turn it on?"

Best Practices for Effective Communication:

✓ Listen carefully – Let the user explain their issue without interruptions.

✓ Ask clarifying questions – "When did this issue start?" "Did anything change recently?"

✅ Stay patient and calm – Even if the customer is upset, your professionalism matters.

✅ Repeat back the problem – "Just to confirm, your Wi-Fi isn't working on all your devices?"

✅ Give clear step-by-step instructions – Use simple language when guiding users through fixes.

Pro Tip:

- Not all users are tech-savvy. If someone struggles to follow instructions, slow down and be patient!

2.   Troubleshooting Etiquette – The Do's and Don'ts

How you troubleshoot affects the customer experience.

Do:

✓ Introduce yourself and explain your role.

✓ Gather information before assuming the issue.

✓ Follow a structured troubleshooting process.

✓ Keep the user updated on what you're doing.

✓ Thank the user for their patience.

Don't:

🚫 Be rude or condescending.

$\oslash$ Assume the customer is clueless.

$\oslash$ Blame the user for the issue.

$\oslash$ Rush through troubleshooting without understanding the problem.

$\oslash$ Ignore security protocols when accessing sensitive data.

Pro Tip:

- If an issue takes longer than expected, communicate progress updates to the customer.

("I'm running a diagnostic now. It'll take about 10 minutes, and I'll update you after that.")

IT Ethics – Doing the Right Thing

IT professionals often handle sensitive data and critical systems. Ethical decision-making is crucial to maintaining trust.

The Core Principles of IT Ethics

✓ Confidentiality – Protect user data from unauthorized access.

✓ Integrity – Be honest about what you know (and don't know).

✓ Responsibility – Follow company policies and security guidelines.

✓ Respect – Treat users, colleagues, and data with care.

Example Ethical Dilemmas:

Dilemma 1: You find out a coworker is using company computers to download illegal content. Do you report them?

Solution: Yes! Misuse of IT resources can compromise security.

Dilemma 2: A customer asks you to reset a coworker's password without authorization.

Solution: Follow proper identity verification before resetting passwords.

Pro Tip:

- If you're ever unsure about an ethical issue, check company policies or consult a supervisor.

Legal Considerations in IT

IT professionals must follow laws related to data protection, privacy, and cybersecurity.

Important IT Laws and Regulations:

Law/Regulation	What It Covers
GDPR (EU)	Protects user data and privacy in Europe.
HIPAA (USA)	Protects medical data and patient privacy.
PCI-DSS	Secures payment and credit card transactions.
CCPA (California)	Gives users control over their personal data.

Real-World Example:

A company loses customer data in a hack. If they didn't properly secure it, they could face legal consequences and fines!

Pro Tip:

- Always follow company policies and industry regulations when handling sensitive data.

Cybersecurity and Ethical Hacking

IT professionals play a big role in cybersecurity. Ethical hackers test systems for vulnerabilities before criminals do.

What is Ethical Hacking?

Ethical hackers (a.k.a. "white hat" hackers) use their skills for good. They find security weaknesses before malicious hackers exploit them.

Example:

A cybersecurity expert tests a company's firewall to ensure hackers can't break in.

Pro Tip:

- Ethical hacking follows strict legal guidelines—hacking without permission is illegal!

Quick Check: Test Your Knowledge

1. What's the most important trait when dealing with customers?

2. How can you make technical troubleshooting easier for a non-tech-savvy user?

3. Name two core principles of IT ethics.

4. Why is data privacy important in IT?

5. What should you do if someone asks you to reset a coworker's password?

Chapter 17

Job Roles, Certifications, and Career Growth – Your Path in IT

So, you've mastered IT fundamentals, earned your CompTIA A+ certification (or you're preparing for it), and now you're wondering—what's next?

What IT job should you aim for? Which certifications will boost your career? How do you grow from entry-level to expert?

This chapter will break down:

✓ Different IT career paths and job roles.

✓ Certifications to level up your skills.

✓ Tips for landing your first IT job and growing in the field.

Entry-Level IT Jobs – Where to Start?
The CompTIA A+ certification is widely recognized as an entry point into IT.

Here are some common starting roles:

Job Title	Typical Salary (USD)	What You'll Do
Help Desk Technician	$40,000 – $55,000	Assist users with software/hardware issues.
IT Support Specialist	$45,000 – $60,000	Troubleshoot systems, manage tickets.
Desktop Support Technician	$50,000 – $65,000	Maintain and repair workstations, printers, etc.
Technical Support Specialist	$45,000 – $65,000	Provide remote and in-person tech support.
Field Service Technician	$45,000 – $70,000	Install, repair, and upgrade IT systems onsite.

Pro Tip:

- Don't stress about the "perfect" first job. Any IT experience builds your resume!

Mid-Level IT Roles – What's Next?

Once you gain 1-3 years of experience, you can specialize in networking, cybersecurity, cloud computing, or system administration.

Job Title	Salary Range	Required Skills
Network Administrator	$60,000 – $85,000	Network troubleshooting, routers, firewalls.
Systems Administrator	$65,000 – $90,000	Managing servers, Active Directory, cloud systems.
Cybersecurity Analyst	$75,000 – $110,000	Threat detection, firewalls, security policies.
Cloud Engineer	$85,000 – $120,000	AWS, Azure, Google Cloud services.
IT Project Manager	$80,000 – $120,000	Managing IT projects, budgets, and teams.

Pro Tip:

- Choose a specialization based on your interests! Love security? Go for cybersecurity. Like networking? Become a Network Admin.

IT Certifications – Which Ones Should You Get?

Certifications validate your skills and increase your salary potential.

Here's a roadmap based on your career path:

Core IT & Help Desk (Entry-Level)

✅ CompTIA A+ – PC repair, troubleshooting (You're here!)

✅ CompTIA Network+ – Networking basics (Great for help desk & network techs)

✅ CompTIA Security+ – Cybersecurity fundamentals (For IT security roles)

Networking & Systems Admin

✅ Cisco CCNA – Networking & routers (Great for Network Admins)

✅ Microsoft Certified: Azure Fundamentals – Cloud computing (For cloud careers)

✅ CompTIA Linux+ – Linux server management

Cybersecurity

✅ CompTIA Security+ – First step into security

✅ Certified Ethical Hacker (CEH) – Learn ethical hacking techniques

✅ CISSP – Advanced security management

Cloud & DevOps

✔ AWS Certified Cloud Practitioner – Amazon Web Services basics

✔ Microsoft Azure Administrator – Azure cloud skills

✔ Google Cloud Associate – Google Cloud skills

Pro Tip:

- If you want to get promoted quickly, stack multiple certifications in one area!

How to Land Your First IT Job – Resume & Interview Tips

Crafting an IT Resume That Gets Noticed

No IT job experience? No problem! Highlight:

✔ Certifications (CompTIA A+, etc.)

✔ IT projects (Home lab, PC builds, network setup, etc.)

✔ Soft skills (Problem-solving, communication, troubleshooting)

Example Entry-Level IT Resume (Without Experience):

John Edward

📍 Location: New York, NY | ✉ john.Edward@email.com | ☎ 555-123-4567

Objective:

CompTIA A+ certified IT professional eager to apply technical troubleshooting skills in a help desk role. Passionate about problem-solving and customer support.

Skills:

✓ PC troubleshooting & repair

✓ Windows & Linux OS setup

✓ Basic networking (TCP/IP, DHCP, DNS)

✓ Customer service & technical support

Certifications:

✓ CompTIA A+ (2025)

Projects:

✓ Built a custom PC and configured dual-boot Linux & Windows.

✓ Set up a home network with a firewall and multiple VLANs.

Experience:

(If no IT job yet, list customer service or retail roles that required problem-solving.)

Pro Tip:

- Keep your resume to one page and focus on skills that match the job!

How to Ace Your IT Interview

Most common IT interview questions:

✅ "Tell me about yourself." – Focus on your IT skills and passion for tech.

✅ "How would you troubleshoot a slow computer?" – Explain step-by-step troubleshooting.

✅ "What would you do if a customer is frustrated?" – Show calm, professional communication skills.

✅ "How do you stay updated in IT?" – Mention tech blogs, YouTube channels, and labs.

Best Places to Find IT Jobs:

✅ LinkedIn – Build a profile and network with recruiters.

✅ Indeed & Glassdoor – Search for "Help Desk" or "IT Support" jobs.

✅ Company Websites – Apply directly to IT jobs at companies you admire.

Pro Tip:

- Don't wait to feel 100% qualified—apply to jobs and learn on the go!

How to Keep Growing in IT – Continuous Learning

Technology changes FAST. Staying updated is crucial for career growth.

Follow IT blogs & YouTube channels:

✓ Linus Tech Tips – Hardware & PC building

✓ NetworkChuck – Networking & Linux tutorials

✓ Cybersecurity Now – Security trends & news

Build a home lab:

✓ Set up virtual machines (VirtualBox, VMware)

✓ Experiment with Linux servers, networking, and security tools

✓ Try cloud services like AWS Free Tier

Join IT communities:

✓ r/CompTIA on Reddit – Certification tips

✓ Spiceworks – IT discussions & troubleshooting

✓ LinkedIn groups – Connect with other IT pros

Pro Tip:

- The best IT professionals never stop learning!

Quick Check: Test Your Knowledge

1. What's a common entry-level IT job after CompTIA A+?

2. What certification should you get next if you want to be a Network Admin?

3. Name two resume tips for landing an IT job.

4. What should you do if you don't feel fully qualified for an IT job yet?

5. Why is continuous learning important in IT?

Chapter 18

Quick Reference Cheat Sheets & Real-World Scenarios

You've covered a lot of ground—from hardware and networking to security and troubleshooting. But let's be real: remembering everything on the spot is tough.

That's why this chapter is your go-to reference guide with:

✓ Quick Reference Cheat Sheets – Summarized key concepts for fast review.

✓ Real-World Scenarios – Practical applications of what you've learned in real IT environments.

Quick Reference Cheat Sheets

1. Basic Computer Hardware Components

Component	Function
CPU (Processor)	Brain of the computer, executes instructions.

RAM (Memory)	Temporary storage for running programs.
HDD/SSD (Storage)	Stores OS, files, and applications.
Power Supply (PSU)	Converts electricity for the computer.
Motherboard	Connects all components together.
GPU (Graphics Card)	Renders images, videos, and gaming graphics.

Pro Tip: SSDs are much faster than HDDs—always recommend SSD upgrades for performance boosts.

2. Essential Windows Commands

Command	Function
ipconfig	Shows IP address and network info.
ping [address]	Checks network connectivity.
chkdsk	Scans and repairs hard drive errors.
sfc /scannow	Scans and fixes system files.
tasklist	Shows running processes.
netstat	Displays network connections.

Pro Tip: Use `ipconfig /flushdns` to clear DNS cache when facing website loading issues.

3. Basic Network Troubleshooting Steps

Step 1: Check physical connections (cables, Wi-Fi).

Step 2: Run `ipconfig` to check IP settings.

Step 3: Use `ping` to test network reachability.

Step 4: Restart the router/modem.

Step 5: Disable/re-enable the network adapter.

Step 6: Check firewall and security settings.

Pro Tip: If a website isn't loading but other sites work, try using Google's public DNS (8.8.8.8, 8.8.4.4).

4. Common Cybersecurity Threats & Solutions

Threat	Solution
Phishing	Don't click on unknown email links.
Ransomware	Keep backups and update antivirus.
Brute-force attacks	Use **strong passwords + MFA**.
Social engineering	Always verify requests before sharing data.

Pro Tip: Always hover over email links before clicking to see the real destination.

Real-World Scenarios & Solutions

Scenario 1: A User Reports "My Computer is Running Slow"

What You Should Do:

Step 1: Open Task Manager (`Ctrl+Shift+Esc`) to check CPU/RAM usage.

Step 2: Run `chkdsk` and `sfc /scannow` to check for disk or system errors.

Step 3: Uninstall unnecessary startup programs (`msconfig` in Windows).

Step 4: Upgrade RAM or switch to an SSD if hardware is outdated.

Solution: In most cases, disabling background programs and upgrading to an SSD speeds up performance.

Scenario 2: No Internet Connection

What You Should Do:

✓ Step 1: Check Wi-Fi or Ethernet cable connections.

✓ Step 2: Restart the router and modem.

✓ Step 3: Run `ipconfig` to check for valid IP address.

✓ Step 4: Flush DNS with `ipconfig /flushdns`.

✓ Step 5: Test internet on another device.

Solution: If the internet works on other devices, the issue is with the PC. If nothing works, call the ISP.

Scenario 3: User Clicked on a Phishing Link

What You Should Do:

✓ Step 1: Immediately disconnect from the network.

✓ Step 2: Run a full antivirus scan.

✓ Step 3: Change all affected passwords.

✓ Step 4: Report the phishing attempt to IT security.

Solution: Educate the user on phishing awareness and enable MFA to prevent future incidents.

www.ingramcontent.com/pod-product-compliance
Lightning Source LLC
LaVergne TN
LVHW051654050326
832903LV00032B/3796